The British Photographer Abroad

The First Thirty Years

Arthur Backhouse

Pots and Pans, at Nice

Albumen print from a waxed paper negative, 1855 214 × 277mm

The British Photographer Abroad

The First Thirty Years

Robert Hershkowitz

Robert Hershkowitz Ltd.

First published 1980 by
Robert Hershkowitz Ltd.
5 Kynance Mews London

ISBN: 09507057 0 5 Hardcover
ISBN: 09507057 1 3 Softcover

Printed by Jayscale Duotone Offset
at the Printing House of
John S. Speight Limited
Parkside Press
Guiseley Yorkshire England

CONTENTS

INTRODUCTION

> "Photographs are more than tales, they are facts endowed with convincing brute force."
> August Salzmann quoted by André Jammes, *French Primitive Photography*

> "The most important photographs of the nineteenth century are surely those first views of remote people and places brought back to the western world by a pioneering generation of expeditionary photographers."
> Alan Thomas, *The Expanding Eye*

Imagine the world virgin before the eye of the camera, waiting to be photographed for the first time.

In January 1839, pre-empting by a single day Arago's address to the Acádemie des Sciences, the journalist Gaucheraud, in an article on Daguerre's marvellous new invention, first raised the issue of foreign travel photography.

> "Travellers may perhaps soon be able to procure M. Daguerre's apparatus, and bring back views of the finest monuments and of the most beautiful scenery of the whole world. They will see how far their pencils and brushes are from the truth."[1]

In the autumn of that year, N. P. Lerebours, optical instrument maker-cum-publisher, commissioned a number of artists and writers to travel from Spain to the Holy Land, equipping them with daguerreotype outfits of his own manufacture. These commissioned daguerreotypes, as well as ones sent from as far away as Moscow and Niagara Falls, provided the imagery for the engravings illustrating his *Excursions Daguerriennes: vues et monuments les plus remarquable du globe,* published in parts from 1840 to 1843. The French tradition of foreign travel daguerreotypes during the 1840's became fabulously strong, reaching as far as Japan and the South Pacific; whereas the role of the British travel daguerreotype was quite limited, with those made and supervised by Dr. Ellis in Italy forming the only coherent group and really belonging to the incunabula of British photography.

The rich tradition of early British foreign travel photography, characterized by its enormous variety and ubiquitous vitality, began, as one might expect, with Talbot, his pictures and his process. The first Britons to take up the implicit challenge of travel photography — doctors, solicitors, men of leisure, men of commerce, clergymen, soldiers, artists and scientists — converged on this medium of expression from a wealth of personal perspectives. They were amateurs all, and needless to say, had no body of photographic images on which to rely as a starting point. The prints of these early amateurs were made from paper negatives taken before 1858, in places as distant as Australia, Burma, Peru, Russia and Egypt.

The aesthetic of early photography is a complicated affair. It has been simply called *primitive,* a term most clearly defined by Sobieszek, meaning an aesthetic of "directness," of "straightforward immediacy."

> "The primitives were fascinated with the mystery and power that an unequivocal rendering of their world would impart."[2]

They convey a sense of the magic they felt in that Talbot's calotype process actually worked. In the work of the *primitives* — this unfortunate term seemingly unavoidable — there is often a roughness or uneveness to the print or some flaw in the negative. (Likewise, in the early 1850's, the first foreign-made wet collodion negatives were inevitably spotted, streaked or smeared.) By 1855 there were a few photographers using paper negatives who transcended the *primitive,* whose work reveals most sophisticated sensibilities, notably Fenton, Greene, Tripe and Backhouse. Their images seem to be as much expressions of the artists' visions as records of the scenes set before them.

The 1850's also witnessed the emergence of the professional travel photographer, who generally produced large series of albumen prints from the faster, sharper wet collodion negatives, to be published in books and/or distributed commercially by the print trade. Frith was the paragon of the new breed, the intrepid photographer overcoming both physical danger and technical difficulty in capturing memorable images that were taken to be truthful representations of the world as it was by an eager Victorian public. In this published work there is a subtle shift in emphasis in the epistemological significance of the photographic image; more than just an aesthetic response to the world, it was also a visual fact, a discrete bit of information within a materialistic, encyclopediac view of the world.

We are only beginning to assess early photography's profound impact on the Victorian view of the world and to describe its locus in an art historical context. Photographic images, particularly from the late 1850's onward, reinforced the attitude(s) of mind which lay behind the imperialist approach to international politics, the positivist, materialist approach to the natural world and a belief in progress through advancing technological development. "The most grandiose result of the photographic enterprise" — the ability to capture on paper visual experience with the presumption of veracity — "is to give us the sense that we can hold the whole world in our heads."[3] Early photographs of foreign lands, available in great quantity and variety to the Victorian public through exhibition and print dealer, have been overlooked and ignored in more recent times.

The publication of this book coincides with an exhibition being held at the Camden Arts Centre in London. If there were world enough, money and time, the exhibition would have been more than six times as large, eight hundred photographs being a proper Victorian-sized show, and the book a complete catalogue. Ideally, water colours, drawings, engravings, lithographs and etchings of similar subject matter would have been included to substantiate the idea of *camera vision* and to isolate the aesthetic of the early photographic print. 1871 is obviously an arbitrary closing date, providing only a truncated view of the whole. Another seven years would have seen the inclusion of Mrs. Cameron's Ceylon portraits, Muybridge's trip to Central America, Burke's coverage of the Second Afghan War, the publication of Woodbury's *Treasure Spots of the World* and Thomson's glorious study of the people and landscape of Cyprus; and surely the evident conclusions to the theme of early British foreign travel photography reside in the work of Evans in France and Ponting in Antarctica, in the first years of this century. Pictures by early French Photographers — let us say prints by Teynard, Du Camp, Le Clerq, Salzmann, Charnay and Tremaux, and daguerreotypes by De Prangey and Baron Gros, to name a few — would have been included, if only to point up the differences between English and French sensibilities.

Except for the isolated example of Charnay in Madagascar in 1863, French expeditionary photography had stopped in its tracks by 1860. (A few Frenchmen did photograph in the Middle East in the 1860's and 1870's, but by this time the Holy Land had been done to death.) From 1860 to 1880, while Great Britain was consolidating and expanding its empire and spheres of influence, France's imperial activity and overseas ambitions were much more modest in scale. Following what might be called an aesthetic version of Gresham's law — that cheap money drives dear money out of circulation — the rise of commercial photography in England and France in the 1860's drove many of the finest practitioners in both countries from the medium; but for the British photographer working abroad, particularly in Asia and the Western Hemisphere, there were still new realms of experience to discover and fix in permanent image.

Plate 1

Dr. Alexander John Ellis
Campanile, Florence
Wholeplate daguerreotype, 1841   165 × 215mm

Plate 2

Dr. Alexander John Ellis
View from the Church of S. Martina
Wholeplate daguerreotype, 1841 215 × 165mm

Plate 3

William Henry Fox Talbot
View of the Boulevards of Paris
Calotype, 1843 188 × 223mm (including margins)

Plate 4

William Henry Fox Talbot
The Pantheon, Paris
Calotype, 1843   198 × 245mm (including margins)

Plate 5

Rev. Calvert Jones
The House of Sallust, Pompeii
Calotype, 1846   195 × 245mm (including margins)

Plate 6

Rev. Calvert Jones

Naples

Calotype, 1846 (right half of panorama) 224 × 187mm (including margins)

Plate 7

Rev. George Bridges

Taormina, Sicily

Calotype, c. 1846 (the man with the sketchpad may be Calvert Jones) 160 × 230mm

Plate 8

Rev. George Bridges
Etna, Sicily
Calotype, c. 1846 197 × 248mm (including margins)

Plate 9

Dr. Claudius Galen Wheelhouse
Seville
Calotype, 1849 188 × 230mm (including margins)

Plate 10

Dr. Claudius Galen Wheelhouse
Interior of the Parthenon
Calotype, 1850   177 × 205mm

Plate 11

Dr. Claudius Galen Wheelhouse
Hall of Columns, Karnak
Calotype, 1850 177 × 205mm

Plate 12

John Shaw Smith
Capitals of the Leper Columns in the Great Hall Karnak
Calotype, 1852 171 × 222mm

Plate 13

John Shaw Smith
Street in Pera, Constantinople
Calotype, 1852 170 × 216mm

Plate 14

Anonymous Scottish Photographer
Pioneer Town in Australia
Calotype, c. 1851 147 × 199mm (including margins)

Plate 15

Robert MacPherson
Coliseum, Rome
Calotype, c. 1850 156 × 201mm

Plate 16

Sir James Francis Dunlop
Coliseum, Rome
Calotype, c. 1850 150×188mm

Plate 17

Anonymous Scottish Photographer
Rouen
Calotype, c. 1850   214 × 272mm

Plate 18

John Stewart
Sauveterre from *Souvenirs des Pyrénées*
Blanquart-Evrard process print, 1852 216 × 302mm

Plate 19

Dr. John McCosh
Artillery in Front of Stone Dragons, Prome
Calotype, 1852 175 × 218mm

Plate 20

Dr. John McCosh
East Vestibule of Great Pagoda, Rangoon
Calotype, 1852 186 × 224mm

Plate 21

Roger Fenton
Post House at Kiev
Salt print from a waxed paper negative, 1852 358 × 280mm

Plate 22

Roger Fenton
Peasant Hut
Varnished salt print from a waxed paper negative, 1852 164 × 210mm

Plate 23

Thomas Sutton

Forum, Rome

Waxed salt print from an unspecified paper negative, c. 1853 186 × 237mm

Plate 24

John Buckley Greene
View in Egypt
Salt print from a waxed paper negative, c. 1854 226 × 296mm

Plate 25

Arthur Backhouse
On the Grand Canal, Venice
Albumen print from a waxed paper negative, 1855 214 × 275mm

Plate 26

Arthur Backhouse
Genoa
Albumen print from a waxed paper negative, 1855 214 × 274mm

Plate 27

Capt. Linnaeus Tripe
Ava, Upper Burma
Calotype, 1855 285 × 345mm

Plate 28

Capt. Linnaeus Tripe
Ruins of Fort Palkod
Lightly albumenized calotype, 1857 249 × 355mm

Plate 29

Capt. Linnaeus Tripe
The Causeway across Vaigai River
Lightly albumenized calotype, 1857 245 × 373mm

Plate 30

Dr. John Murray

Scene near Agra

Albumen print from a calotype negative, before 1858   214 × 343mm

Plate 31

Capt. Henry Dixon

The Temple of Anuntoo Bassa, Orissa

Albumen print from an unspecified paper negative, 1858 220 × 304mm

Plate 32

Capt. T. Biggs
Gol Goomuz
Albumen print, c. 1866, from a calotype negative, c. 1856 215 × 278mm

Plate 33

James Robertson and Felice Beato
Saint Sophia, Constantinople
Albumen print, c. 1858, from a wet collodion negative, c. 1853   305 × 263mm

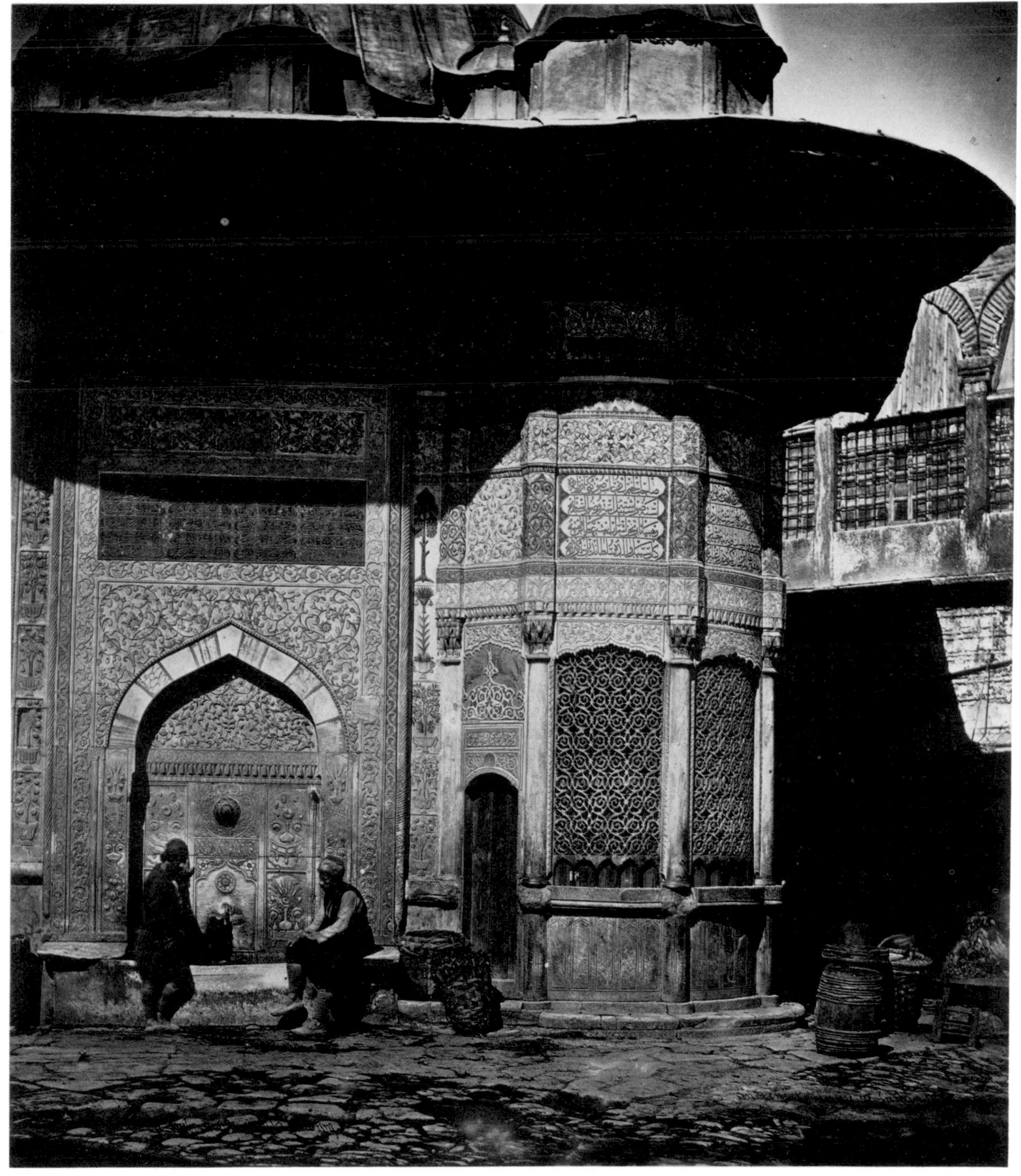

Plate 34

James Robertson and Felice Beato

Scene in Constantinople

Albumen print, c. 1858, from a wet collodion negative, c. 1853 305 × 263mm

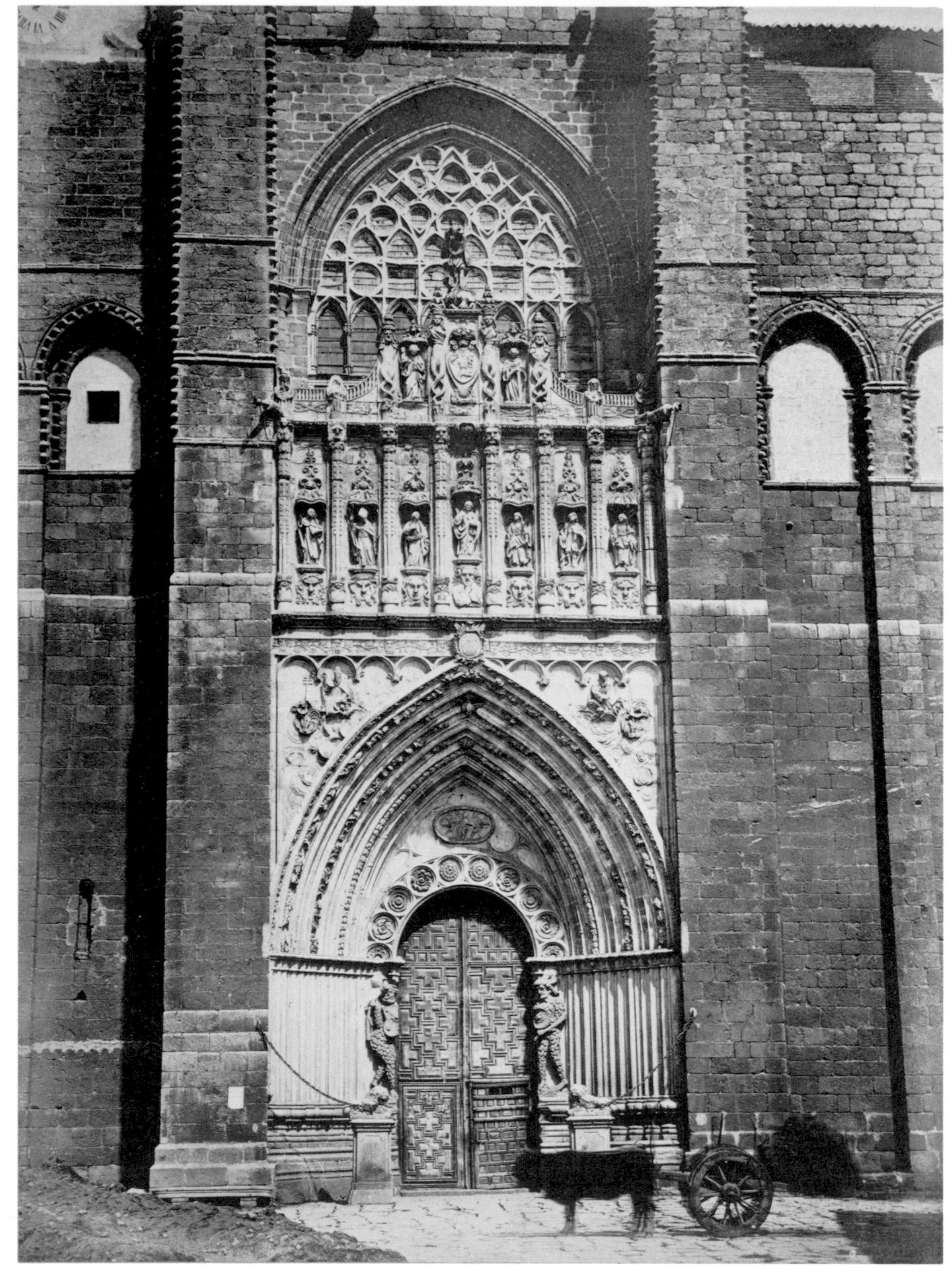

Plate 35

Charles Clifford
South Door, Avila Cathedral
Albumen print from a wet collodion negative, c. 1854 405 × 299mm

Plate 36

Charles Clifford
Court of Lions, Alhambra
Albumen print from a wet collodion negative, c. 1854   310 × 428mm

Plate 37

James Robertson
Propylae, Athens
Albumen print from an albumen on glass negative (?), c. 1855 270 × 370mm

Plate 38

Maxwell Lyte
Le Pont d'Espagne, Pyrenees
Albumen print from a wet collodion negative, 1855 259 × 320mm

Plate 39

Roger Fenton
Mortar Batteries, Crimea
Salt print from a wet collodion negative, 1855 223 × 350mm

Plate 40

Photographer unknown

Aswan, Egypt

Albumen print from a wet collodion negative, 1856 186 × 229mm

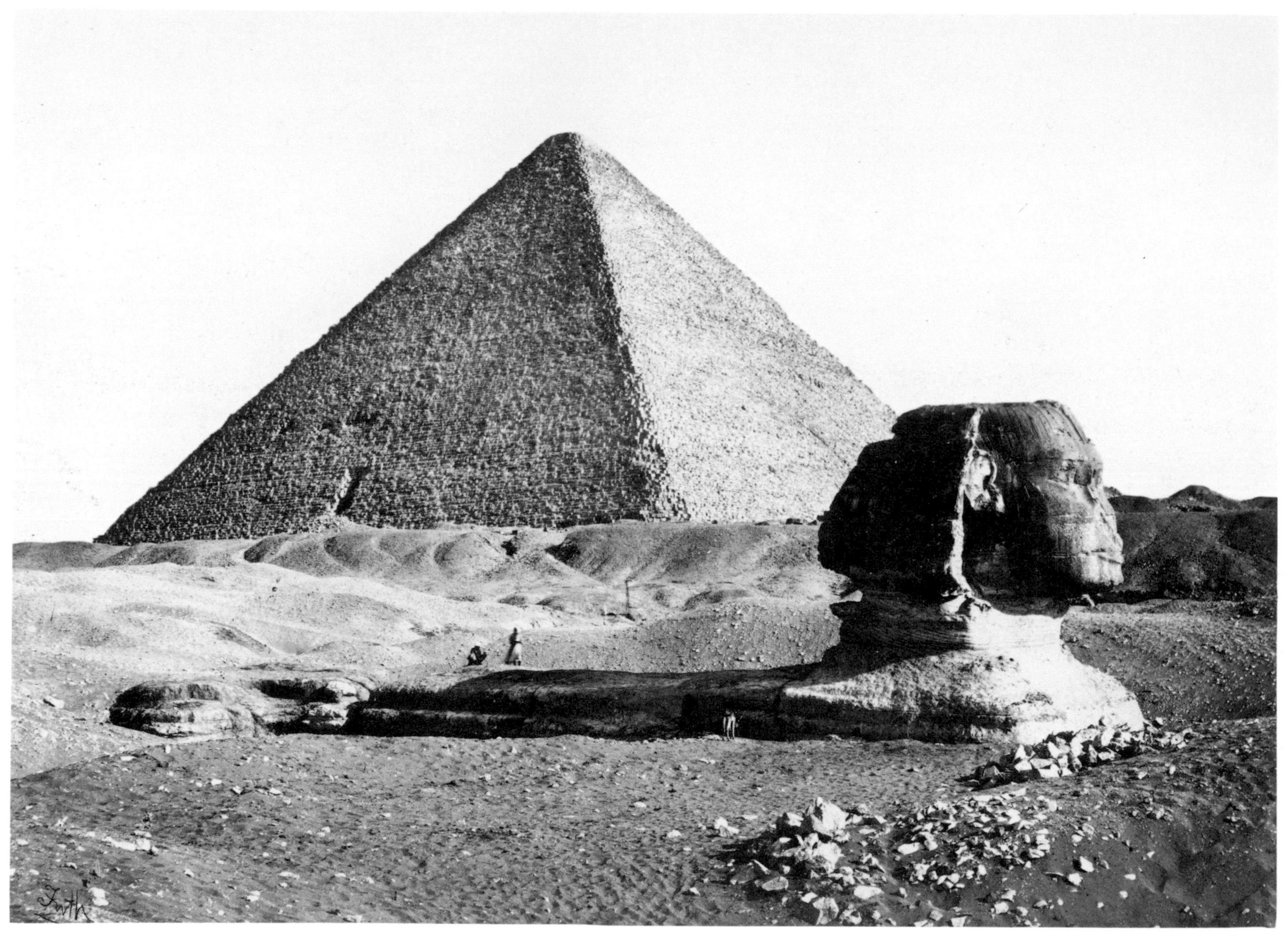

Plate 41

Francis Frith
The Sphinx and Great Pyramid from *Lower Egypt and Thebes*
Albumen print from a wet collodion negative, 1857 160 × 222mm

Plate 42

Francis Frith

Kuom Ombo from *Sinai and Palestine*

Albumen print from a wet collodion negative, 1858 391 × 480mm

Plate 43

Felice Beato

Scene along the Ganges

Lightly albumenized salt print from an albumen on glass negative, 1858 (panel from a panorama) 253 × 304mm

Plate 44

William Johnson and W. Henderson

Brahmin Students of English from *The Indian Amateur's Photographic Album*

Albumen print from a wet collodion negative, 1857 241 × 196mm

Plate 45

Anonymous Soldier of the Royal Engineers
Spokan Indians
Albumen print from a wet collodion negative, c. 1860   131 × 136mm

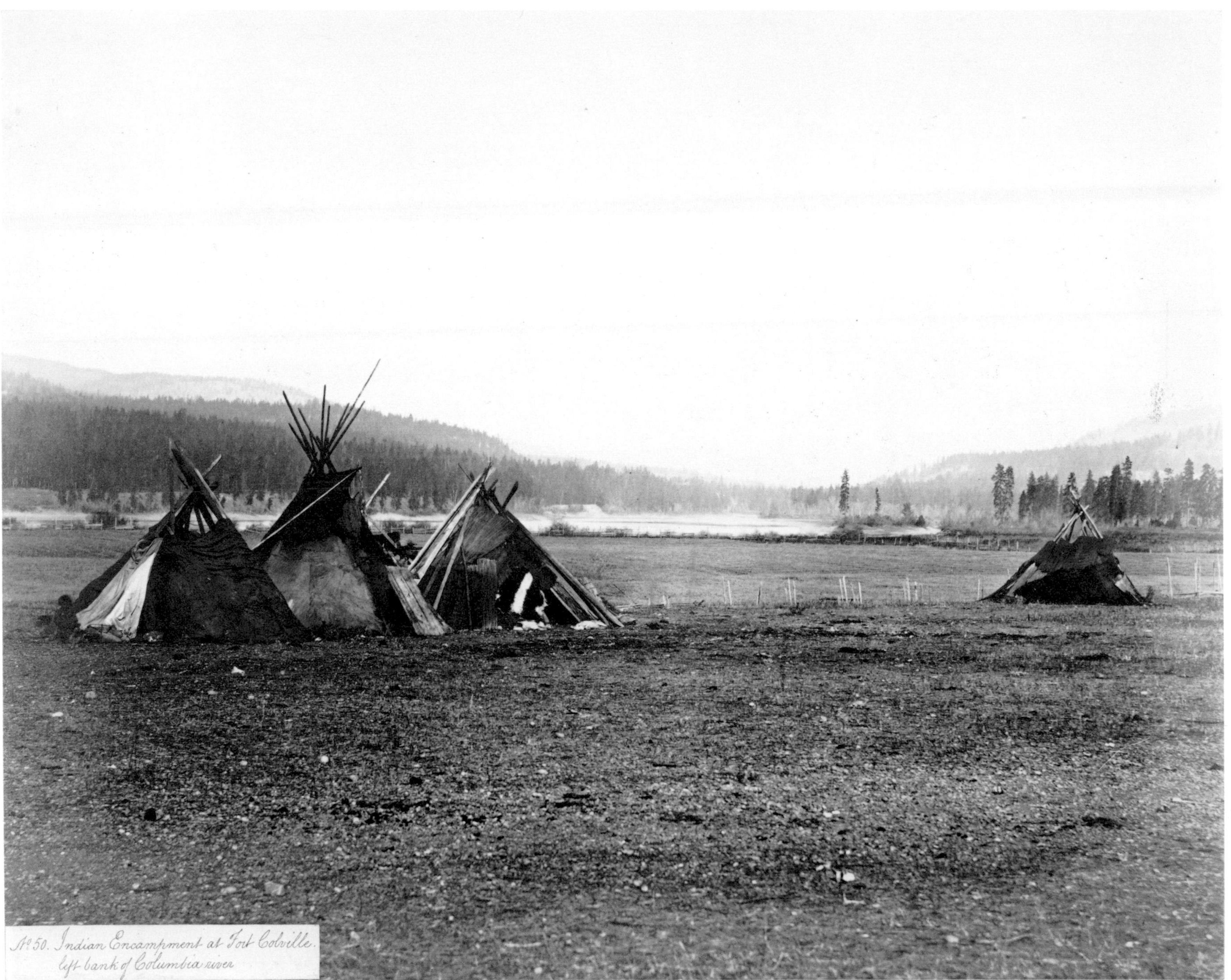

Nº 50. Indian Encampment at Fort Colville.
left bank of Columbia river

Plate 46

Anonymous Soldier of the Royal Engineers
Indian Encampment
Albumen print from a wet collodion negative, c. 1860 212 × 268mm

Plate 47

Ben Mulock
Pequenina
Albumen print from a wet collodion negative, c. 1861 177 × 242mm

Plate 48

Ben Mulock
Building the Railway, Bahia, Brazil
Albumen print from a wet collodion negative, c. 1861 161 × 236mm

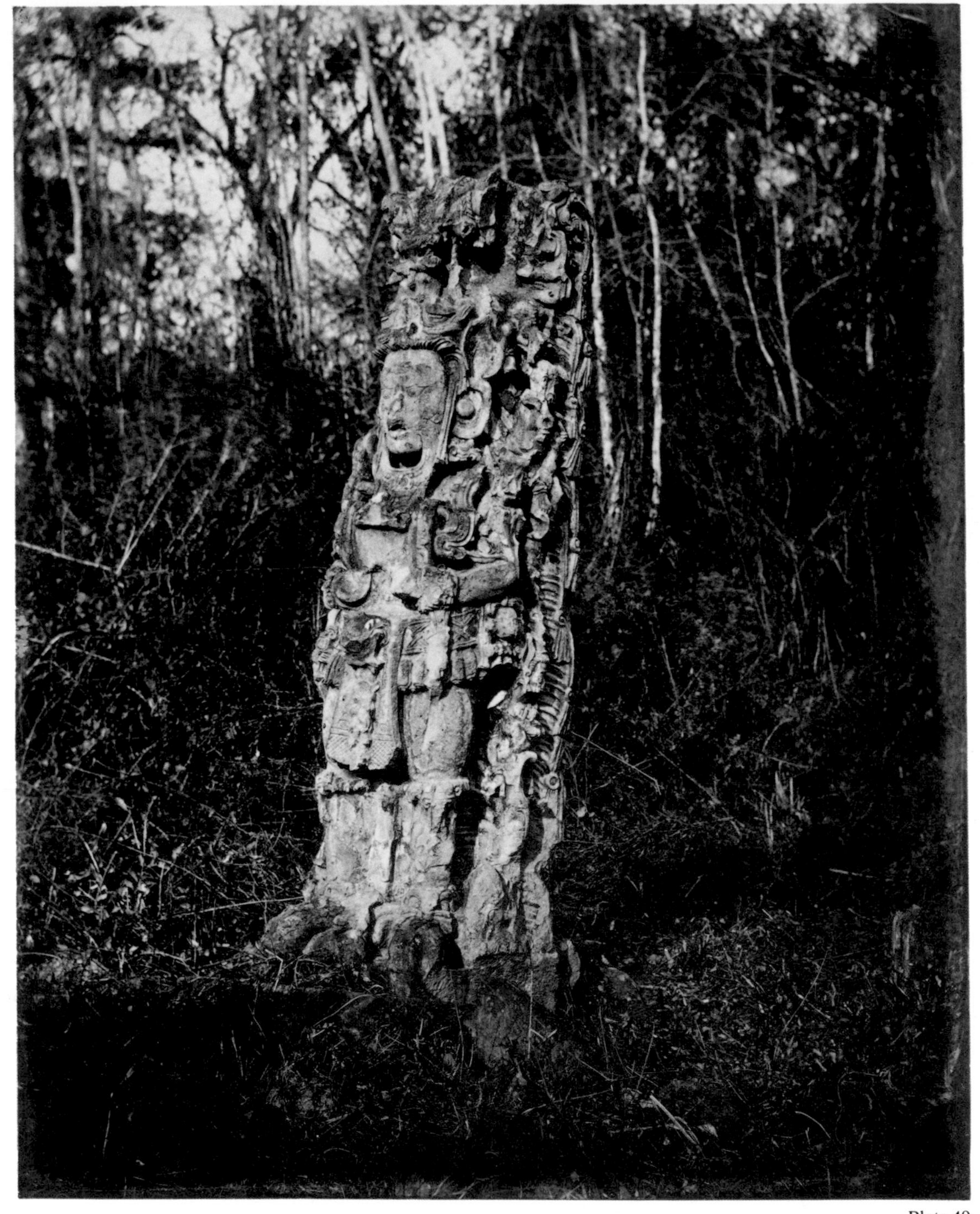

Plate 49

Osbert Salvin
Sculpture at Copan, Honduras
Albumen print from a wet collodion negative, 1863   210 × 168mm

Plate 50

Alexander Gardner
Home of a Rebel Sharpshooter from *Photographic Sketchbook of the War*
Albumen print from a wet collodion negative, 1863 173 × 230mm

Plate 51

Robert MacPherson
Temple of Clitumnus
Albumen print from a wet collodion negative, before 1860   185 × 245mm

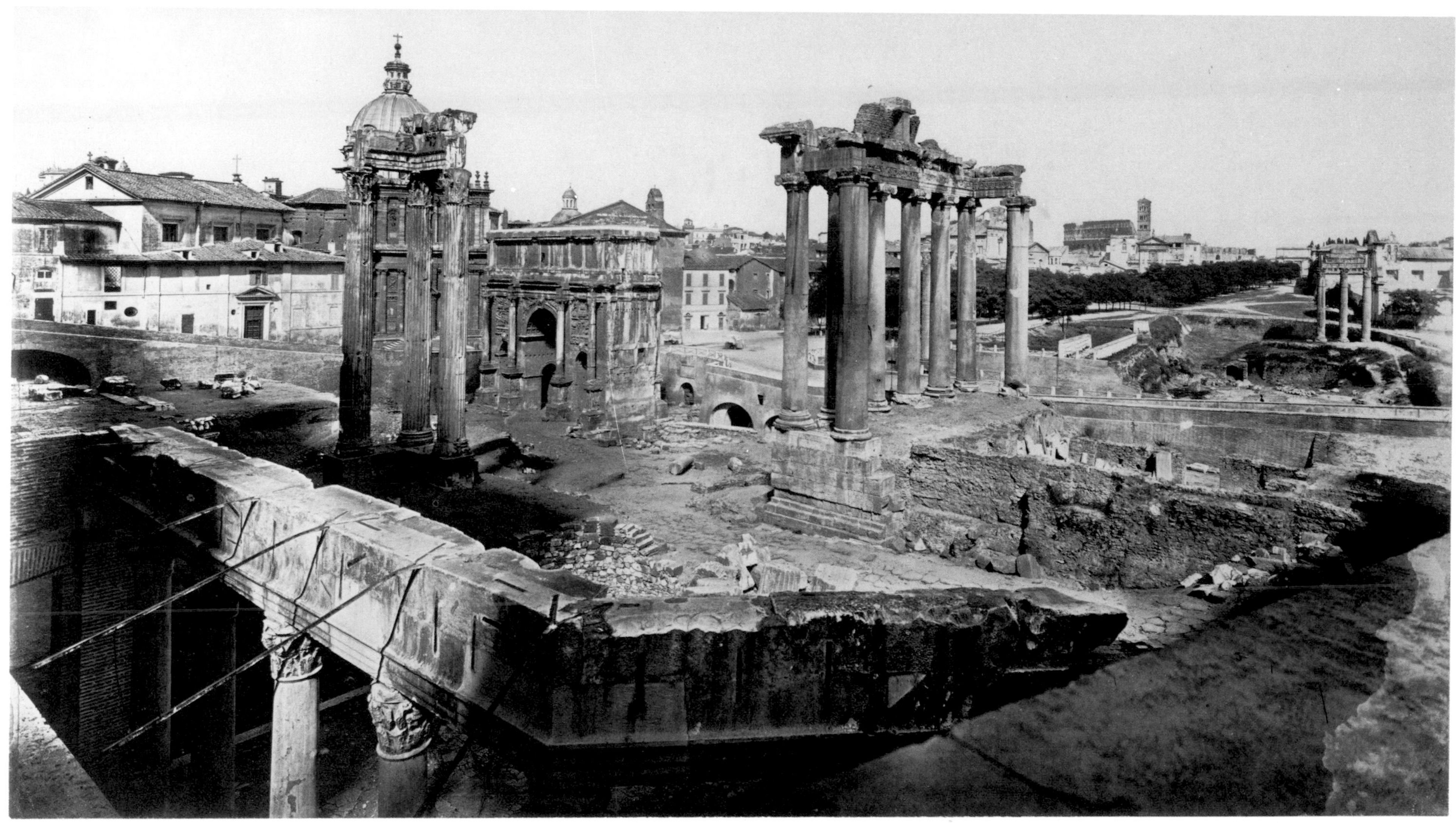

Plate 52

Robert MacPherson
Forum, Rome
Albumen print from a wet collodion negative, before 1863   225 × 245mm

Plate 53

Francis Bedford

Pyramids at Gizeh from *Photographic Pictures taken During a Tour in the East*

Albumen print from a wet collodion negative, 1862 230 × 287mm

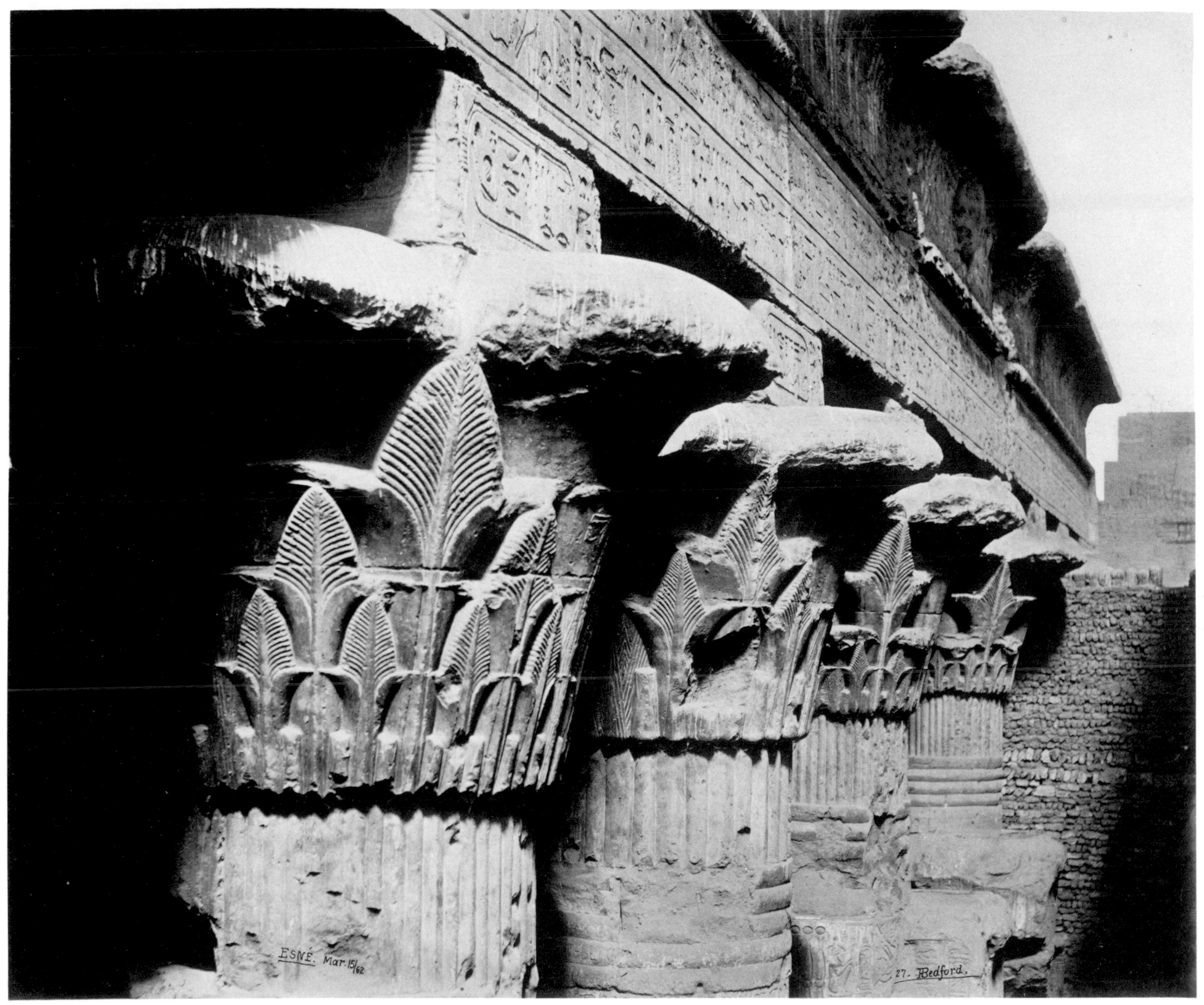

Plate 54

Francis Bedford

Esne, Egypt from *Photographic Pictures taken During a Tour in the East*
Albumen print from a wet collodion negative, 1862 232 × 287mm

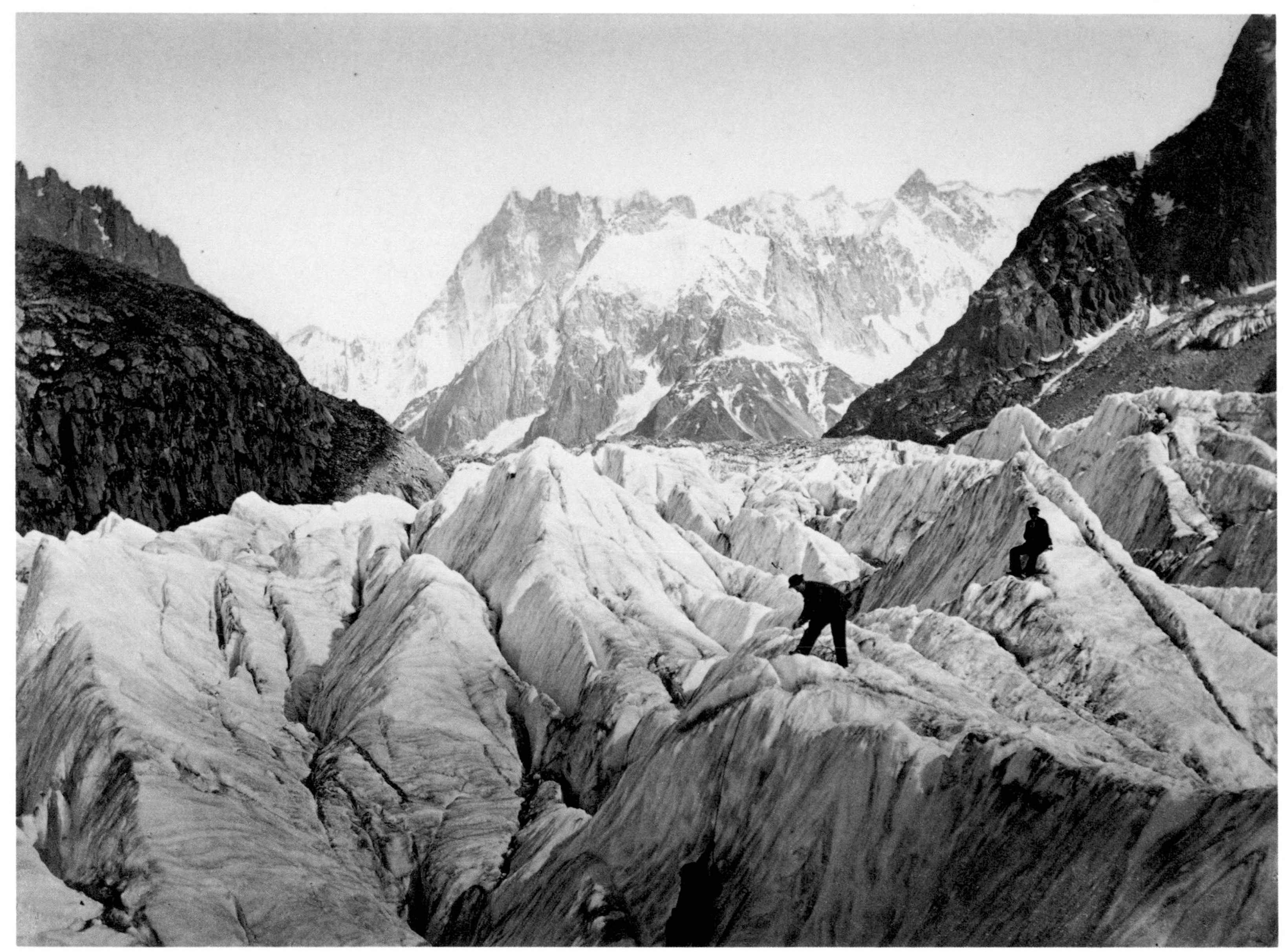

Plate 55

William England
Mer de Glace, Chamonix from *Views of Switzerland and Savoy*
Albumen print from a wet collodion negative, c. 1863 158 × 212mm

Plate 56

William England

Staubbach, Switzerland from *Views of Switzerland and Savoy*

Albumen print from a wet collodion negative, c. 1863 158 × 210mm

Plate 57

William Carrick

Russian Peasants from the series *Simbirsk Scenes*

Albumen prints from wet collodion negatives, c. 1871 138 × 97mm each

Plate 58

Charles Shepherd

Fort Jamrud, Khyber Pass

Albumen print from a wet collodion negative, c. 1865   197 × 287mm

Plate 59

Attributed to Willoughby Wallace Hooper
Low Caste Hindus from *People of India*
Albumen print from a wet collodion copy negative, before 1864 130 × 108mm

Plate 60

Samuel Bourne
Tibetan Lama
Albumen print from a wet collodion negative, c. 1865 225 × 183mm

Plate 61

Samuel Bourne
Manirung Pass
Albumen print from a wet collodion negative, c. 1865   232 × 292mm

Plate 62

Samuel Bourne
Canal in Kashmir
Albumen print from a wet collodion negative, c. 1865 238 × 299mm

Plate 63

Samuel Bourne

Fatehpur Sikri

Albumen print from a wet collodion negative, c. 1865   240 × 295mm

Plate 64

Walter Woodbury and Page

Scene in Java

Albumen print from a wet collodion negative, 1860 190 × 244mm

Plate 65

Felice Beato
Pei-t'ang Fort, August, 1860
Albumen print from a wet collodion copy negative, 1860 246 × 292mm

Plate 66

Attributed to Felice Beato
Scene in China
Albumen print from a wet collodion negative, before 1862 208 × 265mm

Plate 67

John Thomson

Junk

Albumen print from a wet collodion negative, c. 1868 218 × 277mm

Plate 68

John Thomson

British Consulate, Canton

Albumen print from a wet collodion negative, c. 1868 231 × 286mm

Plate 69

Felice Beato
Garden of Teahouse at Hatta from *Photographic Studies of Japan*
Albumen print from a wet collodion negative, before 1868 232 × 288mm

Plate 70

Felice Beato

Nikko from *Photographic Studies of Japan*

Albumen print from a wet collodion negative, before 1868 223 × 228mm

Plate 71

Eadweard Muybridge
Bridal Veil Fall, Yosemite, California
Albumen print from a wet collodion negative, 1871 418 × 530mm

Plate 72

Felice Beato
Mount Fuji from *Photographic Studies of Japan*
Albumen print from a wet collodion negative, before 1868 217 × 297mm

THE BRITISH PHOTOGRAPHER ABROAD:
The First Thirty Years

"Come then ye talented photographers . . . from the five corners of the globe, and let us hear what you are doing and where you have been wandering. Tell us what known and unknown places the camera has penetrated."

Samuel Bourne, "A Photographic Journey through the Himalayas," *British Journal of Photography,* 26/11/1869.

Using Daguerre's original process, Dr. Alexander John Ellis made or had made a large group of wholeplate daguerreotypes, the majority in Rome during 1840-41, one hundred and fifty-eight of which are now happily part of the Science Museum's collection. Following the example of *Excursions Daguerriennes,* Dr. Ellis, a noted classical philologist, intended to publish periodically *Italy Daguerreotyped: a collection of views chiefly architectural engraved after daguerreotypes,* but the plan was abandoned. In a memorandum now in the Science Museum, Dr. Ellis explained his motive: addressing himself in the third person, he wrote:

> "It was solely because [he] could not obtain any views of Rome etc. which he could trust as accurate that he undertook the laborious task of daguerreotyping the country."[1]

The earliest examples were made under Ellis' direction by Achille Morelli and Lorenzo Suscipi, and the later ones, technically and aesthetically superior to those by his Italian assistants, by Dr. Ellis himself, and these often bear wonderfully detailed notes concerning the exposure on the backs of their wooden frames. (Plates 1 and 2).

Very little else has survived.* The daguerreotypes taken in Palestine and Syria by Dr. George Skene Keith, used to illustrate *Evidence of the Truth of the Christian Religion,* a book by his father, the Rev. Alexander Keith, are apparently lost. Apparently lost also are the daguerreotypes made in France by George Edwards and in Italy by Phipps; these are only known by their inclusion in the catalogue for the first exhibition of the Photographic Society in 1853. The only other British travel daguerreotypes extant are those made or supervised by John Ruskin, himself an avid collector. According to Aaron Scharf, Ruskin made daguerreotypes in Switzerland as late as 1856.[2] Ruskin's own work is mingled with his collection presently housed and uncatalogued in the Ruskin Galleries on the Isle of Wight.

*Foreign-made studio daguerreotypes, as by Newlands or Baker of Calcutta or Mackay of Hong Kong, are just beyond the scope of this book.

The Pencil of Nature, Talbot's exemplar book as to the potential uses of the calotype, contains two images of France. Taken from an upper storey window in the Hotel des Douvres, his *View of the Boulevards of Paris,* published in Part I, issued in June 1844, heralded the extraordinary tradition of early British foreign travel photography. (Though travel photography as such was never an issue for Talbot, Gail Buckland suggests that during 1843 he briefly flirted with the idea of publishing a *'photo essay'* on the ornamentation and architecture of French cathedrals.)[3] Maintaining as nearly as possible the exact same pictorial relationships among the parts, Talbot also photographed this view of the boulevards from street level. (Plate 3) The very unpainterly concept of virtually endless variations on a single subject as being a suitable theme for photography was discussed by Talbot in the text accompanying the *Bust of Patroclus,* also in Part I.

In the opening article of the July 1846 issue of *The Art Union,* an unnamed editor made some fanciful speculations regarding the potential uses of the calotype in rather exotic situations, such as locating the watering places during the "systematic exploration of Central Australia," or avoiding those spots "infected with miasmata or malaria" during "the exploration of African Rivers," or indicating "the places where pirates are accustomed to lurk" in the Indian Archipelago, "a new and lucrative field for the extension of British commerce."[4] According to this author, however, the greatest value of the travel calotype is as hand and foot servant to the topographical painter:

> "Painters are not in the present day the most enterprising of travellers; we have had few artists visit the ruins of Babylon or the wilds of Australia; but sun-pictures obtained from thence would enable the artist to delineate such scenes as faithfully as if he had visited the spot; particularly as these sun-pictures would give him . . . some dozen varieties of views."[5]

The Reverend Calvert Jones first brought the calotype to the Mediterranean and the Reverend George Bridges to Greece and to the Holy Land; both were members of Talbot's circle and frequently corresponded with him while working abroad. Jones, a talented water colourist, made numerous calotypes in Rome, Florence, Naples, Malta and Sicily, during his *grand tour* in 1845-46.[6] Jones was the first calotypist to include the human figure, which provided scale in relationship to unfamiliar architecture and generally enlivened the scene. (Plate 5) His two-panel panorama of Naples, onc of the earliest examples of this genre, displays a strong, inventive composition charged with a highly personal sense of subject.

Rev. Calvert Jones, *Naples,* 1846

(Plate 6) Talbot purchased some of Jones' negatives, which were subsequently printed at the Reading Establishment under Hennemann's supervision and then sold in quantity through bookshops and print dealers.

The Reverend Bridges, schooled in the ways of the calotype by Hennemann, Talbot's assistant, and then by Jones in Malta, wandered with camera for seven years, 1846-52, through Italy, Greece, Malta, the Holy Land and Egypt, producing an astonishing seventeen hundred negatives. He had great technical difficulties and relatively few positive prints have survived. (Plates 7 & 8) His plans for publishing came to nothing. He produced prototypes for *The Illustrations of the Acropolis of Athens* and its sequel, illustrated with thirty-six and thirty calotypes respectively; however nothing further came of this project. Another projected publication which did not materialize was *Palestine as it is: a series of photographic views illustrating the Bible,* to have been issued in twenty monthly parts with four prints in each, by Hogarth Press, starting in December 1858.

Rev. George Bridges, *Great Pyramid and Sphinx,* c. 1851

The first Britons to make successful grand photographic tours of Egypt and the Holy Land were Dr. Claudius Galen Wheelhouse and John Shaw Smith. Dr. Wheelhouse, surgeon to a party of young noblemen touring the Mediterranean by yacht, made calotypes in Portugal, Spain and all the eastern Mediterranean countries from Egypt around to Italy. (Plates 9 - 11) His *Photographic Sketches of the Mediterranean,* in the collection of the Royal Photographic Society, an album of albumen prints made from these calotypes, contains picture captions recalling archetypal incidents in the life of the expeditionary photographer: how many photographers, starting with Wheelhouse and ending with Thomson in China thirty years later, were thought to be spies or soul-stealing sorcerers by bewildered, uncomprehending locals? John Shaw Smith, a wealthy Irish aristocrat and amateur archaeologist, made over three hundred calotypes during 1850-52, while touring France, Italy, the Holy Land and Egypt. (Plates 12 and 13) The image of a *Street in Pera, Constantinople,* deliberately, but inexplicably made from two negatives, may well be the earliest known combination print. An album of Smith's Egyptian views, the key item in the collection of The Photographic Society of Ireland, contains albumenized or varnished calotypes; in some of the images the relation of the strange cloudy skies (painted on the negatives) to the monumental architecture of the ostensible subject matter feels distinctly surreal in effect.

Once Talbot had communicated the details of his process to Sir David Brewster, Edinburgh soon became a hive of photographic activity, and in the early 1840's, "when the excitement was at its highest . . . the Calotype Club was formed."[7] In the late 1880's, John Millar Gray, then curator of the Scottish National Portrait Gallery, described the contents of two club albums, one of which survives in the Edinburgh Public Library; included are varnished calotypes of

> "foreign scenes in Antwerp, Rouen, and Rome, and an excellent series of the rich domestic architecture of Ghent; while one member penetrated to South America and gives us renderings of the quays and public buildings in Lima."[8]

This extant album of one hundred and twenty-three calotypes includes three by MacPherson in Rome, fifteen by Sir James Francis Dunlop — apparently the teacher of MacPherson — primarily in Rome and Malta, one of the later being dated 1848, and two by George Moir in Belgium. The collection of the Scottish National Portrait Gallery contains loose prints of foreign travel views by early club members: scenes of Rome — identified as the same images are credited in the extant album — by MacPherson and Dunlop, anonymous calotypes of Australia and, corresponding apparently to images in the lost club album as described by Gray, views of Rouen and Lima. (Plates 14-17)

One of the founding members of the Edinburgh Calotype Club, John Stewart, lived in Pau in the French Pyrenees during the 1850's. Of Stewart's landscapes, a few of which were shown in the earliest photographic exhibition in London in 1852, his brother-in-law, John Herschel wrote in a note to the catalogue, that the

> "representations of superb combination of rock, mountain, forest and water . . . are among the most exquisite in their finish and artistic in the general effect of any specimen of that art which I have seen."[9]

Stewart was a member of the Société Française de Photographie and his work was published by Blanquart-Evrard in *Souvenirs Photographiques* and *Souvenirs des Pyrénées* in the early 1850's. (Plate 18) Stewart, along with Maxwell Lyte, another British resident of Pau and member of the S.F.P., and Thomas Sutton, whose *Souvenir de Jersey* was published by Blanquart-Evrard, were among the principal agents who kept the flow of information about the latest developments in photographic chemistry and technology moving across the channel in both directions. (Plates 38 and 23)

J. B. Greene, the young English archaeologist who lived in Paris and was a founder member of the Société Française, while accompanying a French expedition, produced magnificent calotypes of Egypt, some of which were published by Blanquart-Evrard in an album titled *Le Nil. Monuments, Paysages. Explorations Photographiques.* A planned second publication was cancelled due to Greene's untimely death at age twenty-four in 1856. A comparison of the *primitive* straightforward Egyptian images of Wheelhouse and Smith with those by Greene, immediately reveals a mastery of the medium and sophistication of vision undreamed of by his predecessors.

A comparison of the Burmese calotypes by Dr. John McCosh (plates 19 and 20), surgeon to the Fifth Bengal Artillery Battery, made in Rangoon during the Second Burma War in 1852 with those made by Captain Linnaeus Tripe of the Royal Engineers, taken in Ava, Upper Burma in 1855, displays a parallel leap in vision. (Plate 27) Likewise, in 1854-55, Arthur Backhouse, during a grand tour of Italy, Switzerland and France, produced work far surpassing any previous British effort on the continent, nine examples of which were shown in the Photographic Society's second annual exhibition in 1855.

Whereas earlier travel photographers were satisfied with simply a dark, even print from a well focused, adequately exposed and properly developed negative, by the mid-1850's the more gifted photographers, whose consistently flawless prints suggest that technical mastery of the medium was no longer at issue, exploited the qualities of the print to individual ends and were often more daringly expressive in their compositions. By devoting roughly two-thirds of the image to blank sky, one seventh to the ostensible subject and one fifth to sand, seen as texture, and this thinning out to next to nothing at the bottom, floating what little image there was, J. B. Greene transformed the Egyptian landscape into fabled mirage, contrary to the virtual consensus among early photographers to stress the eternal monumentality of its architecture. (Plate 24)

Though Captain Tripe's job as a Royal Engineers' photographer was primarily to document archaeological monuments and ancient sculpture, his calotypes made in Burma in 1855 and in southern

India on behalf of the Madras Presidency, 1857-58, are equally concerned with mood, light and atmosphere, as the *Remains of Fort Palkod,* the image freed of all apparent architectural significance, clearly suggests. (Plate 28) In most of Tripe's pictures the vertical accents are stressed, giving rhythm and resonance to the image; in *The Causeway across Vaigai River,* Tripe laid bare the bones of this idea. (Plate 29) His prints, so gorgeously rich in texture and opulent in colour — often purple, red-violet brown, pink — further express the romantic dream of the exotic East, a myth so fashionable in Victorian London.

Confident that his albumen prints from waxed paper negatives, with their richly modulated continuous tones, would convey the genuine presence of light, Arthur Backhouse made the flickering passages of light and warm shadow moving across the facades, rather than the architectural matter, the real subject of his views in Genoa and Venice. (Plates 25 and 26) All of Backhouse's images display an extraordinary sense of flow among the constituent parts, especially in comparison to work in the *primitive* vein. His *Pots and Pans, at Nice,* an elegant, witty still life, has subtle blend of classicism and modernity, reminiscent of the spirit in Morandi's paintings. Backhouse played off matte versus glazed pottery surfaces and the smoother pottery against the rough stucco wall and gravelled foreground. The arrangement of the objects was deliberately ambiguous in the number of suggested readings, with the broom, a motif quoted from Talbot's *Open Door,* thrown in for good measure. (Frontispiece)

Between the combined aesthetic of men like Greene, Tripe and Backhouse, in which the world was seen (more or less) as the observer willed, and the more direct vision of the *primitives* lay a gulf which somehow only Fenton seemed to span. The visual syntax of the British *primitive* photographer abroad was basically geometric, with many aspects of the image reduced to shapes read in a plane, a tendency further emphasized by the extreme flatness of the early salt print. (In a salt print, the image is in the paper and in an albumen print, it is on it.)* In Fenton's earliest extant body of work — the Russian images of 1852, made while accompanying his friend and fellow photographer, the engineer, Charles Vignoles, who was commissioned to build a bridge across the Dneiper at Kiev — the sense of geometry became a relentless, self-conscious principle, something spiritual, while the *camera vision* remained straightforward, direct. His images record the discovery of abstract structures in the visual world of landscape and architecture which correspond to an idealized intellectual order, and as such are metaphors for the revelation of mind's place in nature; they display that "blessed rage for order, . . ./The maker's rage to order the words of the sea," in the words of Wallace Stevens from his poem, *The Idea of Order at Key West,* probably the best guide to Fenton's early muse. *The Peasant Hut* is divided into two nearly identical interlocking shapes, a light area of sky and distant snowy landscape and a darker area of foreground incident and the rudest rural architecture, suggestive of a perfect balance between form and space, mass and void, plenitude and emptiness. (Plate 22) Likewise, the *Russian Post House* is divided into two distinct halves; in the left half a wood frame building is seen in perspective with dramatically receding diagonals, and in the right half, a similar building is seen head on: it is as if we are looking at the same building from two different points of view, as in an architect's drawing. (Plate 21) In terms of the history of picture making, Fenton's awareness that the solution to the problem of translating the three dimensional world into a two dimensional image lay in absolute control of composition prefigured Cezanne's more systematic voyagings.

In Russia Fenton used waxed paper negatives, and in the Crimea, in 1855, the wet collodion process, made public by Frederick Scott Archer in 1851. Similarly by 1855, Charles Clifford, in his studies of Spanish architecture, had abandoned the calotype in favour of wet collodion. By 1860 the choice was unanimous, bar MacPherson who used the dry collodion process. The last Britons to use paper negatives abroad were Benjamin Brecknell Turner in Belgium in 1858 and a host of photographers in India, including Major Tytler, Captains Tripe, Biggs and Dixon and Drs. Pigou and Murray, each of whom obtained superb results between 1857-59. (An article in the *Photography Journal* of June 1860 suggests that Captain Biggs was using calotype negatives in India at that late date.) The ever accelerating transition to wet collodion in the 1850's was accompanied, virtually in tandem, with the development of professional foreign travel photography. With precious few exceptions, the historic significance of views by amateurs after 1860, however idiosyncratically interesting, pales in comparison to the commercially produced

*In comparing Wheelhouse's salt and albumen prints made from the same negatives, the albumen prints, made at least a few years later, are invariably richer in colour infinitely more able to render a truly continuous tone, suggesting more strongly the actual presence of light, and seem more sophisticated, less *primitive.*

and distributed views by professionals. Demand was further stimulated in the 1860's by the rise of commercially organized tours of the continent, whose members bought photographic prints as we buy postcards.

We are told by Minor White, that

> "the primitives worked with the photograph innocently or naively, . . . in the amazement at its powers to reflect the detailed minutiae of surface, volume and light,"[10]

an observation which rings true for the large format architectural views made in Spain by Charles Clifford and in Turkey by Robertson and Beato, c. 1853, the earliest examples — except, perhaps, for some calotypes by Jones — of British professional travel photographs. Clifford, a resident of Madrid, member of the Société Française and official photographer to Queen Isabella, exhibited his Spanish views in the Photographic Society's first exhibition in 1854 and in the Paris Photographic Salon of 1856 and published them in two works, *Vistas del Capricho* and *Voyage en Espagne,* the second to contain reputedly about four hundred prints. (Plates 35 and 36)

As even some of the earliest Turkish negatives of 1853 are signed "Robertson & Beato photog.," it is difficult to assess the respective roles of James Robertson, chief engraver to the Imperial Mint in Constantinople, and his Venetian born assistant, Felice Beato, who became a naturalized British citizen. (Plates 33 and 34) They had first met and made calotypes together in Malta in 1850[11]. Beato had a fabulous adventure-filled career: he worked extensively in the eastern Mediterranean, including the Crimea after Fenton's departure in June 1855, and though often credited alone, perhaps with Robertson again, in India in 1858, in the wake of the Lucknow Mutiny. (Plate 43) Summoned by the challenge of the Opium War, Beato joined the Anglo-French expedition in China in 1860 and then worked in Japan from 1862-68.

Commissioned by the Manchester publisher, Thomas Agnew, to produce a set of commercially viable views of the war zone, Fenton, under royal patronage and with the aid of the Secretary of War, ventured to the Crimea, arriving there in March, 1855. In his three active months, before succumbing to cholera, he made over three hundred and sixty negatives, many imperfect due to the difficulties of manipulating the wet collodion in the hot, dusty climate. Well posed, artful studies of individuals and groups dominate the series in number, none of which manifest the sense of horror so vehemently expressed in his letters home. (Plate 39) The scenes of Balaclava Harbour and the minimal landscapes, especially *Valley of the Shadow of Death,* are the most powerful images in the series. Though the work was exhibited and available in London, Manchester and Paris, the project was not a financial success, and a large stock of the photographic prints were put up at auction by the publishers.

The premier entrepreneural photographer was Francis Frith, whose views of the Holy Land and Egypt, made during three separate expeditions in the late 1850's, then published and republished, are unsurpassed in quantity and quality. (Plate 41) Frith's Reigate studio produced "more than 2,000 copies . . . from each of the *negatives*" for the two volume *Egypt and Palestine,* published by James Virtue, 1858-1859; "and the originals . . . as perfect as ever," a four volume set, — *Egypt, Sinai and Palestine, Lower Egypt and Thebes, Sinai*

James Robertson, *Valetta, Malta,* c. 1855

and Palestine and *Upper Egypt and Ethiopia* — including previously unpublished work from the third expedition, was issued by William McKenzie, c. 1863.[12] *Sinai and Palestine,* containing twenty mammoth albumen prints from second expedition negatives, published by James Virtue, c. 1861, is unquestionably Frith's *magnum opus.* In spite of the terrible working conditions, Frith's negatives are virtually flawless, especially in comparison to those of Robertson and Beato, Clifford and Fenton. Frith's mammoth plates were the perfect vehicle to express the monumentality of ancient Egyptian architecture; in *Kuom Ombo* there is an implicit equation between the sculptural, massive presentation of the subject and the subject itself. (Plate 42)

By 1860 Frith's work set the standard for published series of photographic views of foreign lands. Other noteworthy exponents of this genre were: Francis Bedford, whose *Photographic Pictures Taken During a Tour in the East,* made while accompanying the Prince of Wales, was published in 1862; Robert MacPherson, who

"The Prince of Wales' visit to Egypt: His Royal Highness examining the negatives taken by Mr. Bedford, photographist, at Philae" — engraving from the *Illustrated London News,* May 10, 1862

issued a list of over three hundred of some of his available Roman views in 1863; Bourne and Shepherd, whose catalogue of 1866 offered over 1,500 Indian views; Felice Beato, whose *Photographic Studies of Japan* was published by the Japan Gazette Office in Yokohama in 1868; and John Thomson, who in 1873 issued *Foochow on the River Min,* illustrated with carbon prints, and *Illustrations of China and its People,* in four volumes, with two hundred images printed in collotype. The publication of hundreds of photographs on a single theme, each image being a discrete visual fact within an encyclopediac view of the whole, is perfectly consonant with the positivist philosophy, so dominant in nineteenth century thought, wherein,

> "tiny but significant facts, fully described and minutely recorded, have given us the material of present day science,"[13] and that "each fact was to be regarded as a thing capable of being ascertained by a separate act of cognition . . . independent of all the rest and independent of the knower. The historian and scientist must pass no judgement on the facts; he must only say what they were."[14]

Without having to leave the comforts of a Victorian parlour, MacPherson's photographs gave one Rome, Frith's, Egypt and the Holy Land, Bourne's and Shepherd's, India. Images of almost the entire world were or were soon to be available for the imperialist imagination to contemplate and possess, as photographers documented the museum of the world. (Whereas the aesthetic of the 1850's was shaped by the dialogue between subject matter and qualities of print and process, in the 1860's only the pictorialism of alien topography mattered.)

Some photographic series by British born professionals working abroad were produced primarily for local consumption. Three Scottish emigrants, William Carrick, William Notman and Alexander Gardner, who had distinguished careers abroad, had their first exposure to photography in Scotland. Carrick's studio was in St. Petersburg, producing mainly cartes-de-visite and cabinet cards, the standard fare of the commercial portrait photographer. *Simbirsk Scenes,* photographed four hundred miles east of Moscow in the summers of 1871 and 1872, providing wonderful glimpses into the village life of Russian peasants, was his most significant body of images.[15] (Plate 57) Notman, based in Montreal, was the leading

William Notman, *Moose Hunting: the Breakfast,* 1866

publisher of photographic prints in Canada in the second half of the nineteenth century. He was designated official photographer to the Prince of Wales during his Canadian visit of 1860; and later that year published over five hundred stereographs — views primarily around Montreal, especially of the newly opened engineering marvel, the nearly two mile long Victoria Bridge, and of Niagara Falls — examples of which were enthusiastically received in London.

Having started his own business in 1862, after leaving Matthew Brady's studio, Alexander Gardner became photographer to the Ordnance Department of the Army. In 1865 Gardner published a *Photographic Sketchbook of the War* — the two volumes illustrated with one hundred albumen prints, the images primarily by O'Sullivan, but with some by Gardner himself — one of the most important documents of the American Civil War. (Plate 50) Later in the decade, Gardner was hired by the Union Pacific Railroad to record the progress of construction. Another British photographer working in the western United States was Eadweard Muybridge, a resident of San Francisco. While being treated for a back injury in his native England in the early 1860's, he learned

> "the skills of a professional photographer, and his early work suggests the influence of the masters of British topographical photography — Francis Frith, G. W. Wilson and Francis Bedford."[16]

In the late 1860's he photographed around San Francisco, in Yosemite Valley and in Alaska. His deliberately complex, romantic, mammoth views of Yosemite, published by Bradley and Rulofson in 1872, were his finest pictorial work. (Plate 71)

Eadweard Muybridge, *Chinatown, San Francisco,* c. 1865

Two British photographers who worked in Latin America in the early 1860's were Ben Mulock and Osbert Salvin; unfortunately little is known about either. Mulock documented the building of the Bahia and San Francisco Railway, Bahia Province, Brazil in 1860-61. Everything about this series — the prints numbering in the hundreds, each crisp and perfect, the images strong and inventive — suggests the work of a professional employed by the builders of the railway. (Plates 47 and 48) Osbert Salvin was an archaeologist who documented the Mayan sculpture at Copan in Honduras; stereographs from this series were published by Smith and Beck in London in 1863. (Plate 49)

Obviously, a great deal does not fit comfortably into any of the previous categories, most notably the considerable body of work produced by soldiers; and the photographer-soldiers of the Royal

Ben Mulock, *Rio Johannes, Temporary Bridge,* 1861

Osbert Salvin, *Jaguar, Copan, Honduras,* 1863

Engineers form a fascinating story unto themselves. Photographs of St. Petersburg and Moscow made by Sergeant Mack, R.E., in conjunction with the coronation of Tsar Alexander and views of Singapore by Corporal Miliken, R.E., were shown in the Photographic Society's major annual exhibition in 1858. During the Canadian Boundary Expedition of 1859-1860, two anonymous members of the Royal Engineers produced more than one hundred images, providing a rare glimpse of the Indians of British Columbia. (Plates 45 and 46) Photographs by Sergeant McDonald, R.E., were incorporated into the *Ordnance Survey of Jerusalem,* published in 1865. And approximately six Royal Engineers' photographers accompanied the army conducting the campaign in Abyssinia in 1869, an example of Victorian military extravagance, the use of an elephant to squash a fly.

However, the greatest single contribution by photographer-soldiers was in India, documenting in detail the multitude of major archaeological monuments, especially the published architectural photographs by Captains Gill, Dixon, Tripe, Biggs, Lyon and Impey and Dr. Pigou. Other military photographers of note were Major Tytler, pupil of Beato and Murray, who, with his wife, made over five hundred calotypes in 1858, recording the scars inflicted by the Lucknow uprising; Captain Melville Clarke, whose *From Simla through Ludac and Cashmere* was published in 1862; and Captain Willoughby Hooper, one of the few photographers to record images of servants and lower caste Hindus.

As commercial, amateur, military and governmental projects often entwined, by viewing some of the developments in a given region, say Bombay, the focus of greatest activity in the 1850's and early 1860's, one can get a sense of the complex context of early photography in India. Captain Barr was elected the first president of the Bombay Photographic Society in 1854, and by 1855, the society was publishing its own journal and had more than two hundred and fifty members. Under the patronage of the society, in 1857, founding members and commercial photographers, William Johnson and W. Henderson, produced a monthly periodical, *The Indian Amateurs' Photographic Album,* with three prints per issue, featuring a series called *Costumes and Characters of Western India,* the earliest published ethnographic study. (Plate 44) In 1863, Johnson, now a civil servant, produced *Oriental Races and Tribes: Residents and Visitors of Bombay,* illustrated with sixty-one photographs. Captain Biggs was appointed the first official photographer to the Bombay Presidency and in 1855 was succeeded in that post by Dr. Pigou, an army surgeon, in 1857. Albumen prints made from Biggs' calotype negatives were used by the Committee of Architectural Antiquities of Western India in 1866 to illustrate *Architecture at Beehapoor* and *Architecture at Dharwar and Mysore,* though the majority of pictures in the second book are by Dr. Pigou. (Plate 42)

Gray, *The Photographist's Elephant,* 1856

The twin themes of ethnographic and architectural imagery, exemplified by these developments in Bombay, were each expanded and centralized under the direction of the first Governor General,

Lord Canning, an enthusiastic patron of photography. The culmination of the official interest in ethnography was the publication of *The People of India,* an eight volume set with four hundred and sixty-eight pictures by fifteen photographers, issued by the India Office in London and edited by J. Forbes Watson and J. K. Kaye, using copy prints of images in Canning's collection. (Plate 59) Lord Canning appointed General Alexander Cunningham head of the newly established Central Directorate of Archaeology in 1861. After a decade of haphazard progress, relying on volunteers, (with Cunningham himself returning to England for a while in 1866), "the Government of India resolved to re-establish a central authority for archaeological work and offered the post of Director-General to General Cunningham."[17] Incorporating much work of the 1860's along with more recent developments, *The Reports of the Archaeological Survey of India,* running to twenty-three volumes published

Photographer Unknown, *Hunting Scene in India,* c. 1868

between 1871-1887, represents the culmination of the official interest in architecture and archaeology.

From the teeming ghats along the Ganges in Benares, to the idyllic waterways of Kashmir, from desolate mountain passes high in the Himalayas to remote aboriginal villages in the southern hills, Samuel Bourne, between 1863 and 1870, made more than twenty-five hundred negatives: of the hundreds of photographic interpretations of India, his was the finest and most complete. (Plates 61 - 63) Incidents, like his waiting, half-frozen, hours on end, for the clouds to break, to expose a single negative, which appeared in autobiographical accounts of two Himalayan excursions, published serially in the *British Journal of Photography,* have made his raw courage,

Bourne and Shepherd, *Mandalay,* c. 1869

determination and perfectionist aesthetic legendary, projecting the image of the photographer as artist-hero. In all conditions Bourne was the meticulous master of his craft; his ability to capture cloudy skies in treacherous conditions was a technical mystery to his contemporaries. Though the corpus of his work is massive, each and every view is carefully considered. Though famous primarily as a photographer of landscapes and architecture, he was equally at home in the studio, as his intense direct portrait of a *Tibetan Lama,* not

Samuel Bourne, *Kathmandu, Nepal,* c. 1867

unlike an Irving Penn in presentation, suggests. (Plate 60) He was equally energetic as a publisher; in 1870, the year he returned to England, the firm of Bourne and Shepherd issued a catalogue of over two thousand views, available from agents in at least ten cities in India.

India for Beato represented the mid-point of a long, complex career. He had gone there in 1858 upon receiving news of the Lucknow Mutiny, but arrived after the insurrection had been put down. Pursuing his ambition as a *war photographer,* he left India in 1860, joining the Anglo-French punitive expedition against the Chinese. His most significant images of the Second Opium War involved the capture of the Taku Forts, the backbone to the defence of the imperial capital, Peking. In *Fort Pei-t'ang, August, 1860* (Plate 65), he mastered the expressive distribution of figures throughout the picture space, a recurring concern since the early work with Robertson in Constantinople in 1853. (One suspects that in some of the scenes showing the aftermath of battle, Beato directed coolies to place corpses in the pictorially required positions.)

The strongest Chinese images sensationalized the horrors of war; the finest Japanese pictures presented a vision of great tranquility, in which man was at peace with his neighbour and in harmony with the natural world.* In *The Garden at Hatta,* the figures, placed to echo its rhythms, were at one with the garden — a garden of great incident and invention, in which each rock, each shrub, each tree strongly projected its unique identity — and were at one with each other and at one within themselves. (Plate 70) *Nikko* was a more open, less confined expression of this sensibility. (Plate 69)

John Thomson, another far-adventuring Scot, provided the most comprehensive view of life in China, based on his extensive travels inland and along the coast, between 1868-1872. Prior to his Chinese years, he had a great deal of experience as a photographer in Asia, having worked in Penang, Siam and Cambodia (the archaeologically oriented *The Antiquities of Cambodia* appeared in 1867) and having shared a studio with his brother in Singapore. Thomson, like Beato, had a keen eye for pure landscape; and both sought a naturalistic integration of figure and landscape. Thomson's humanist perspective, however, was unique: he systematically portrayed an entire society, from beggar and coolie to prince, and documented regional facial characteristics. He developed the genre in which models were involved in some social activity on which the camera eavesdropped, which became the basis for his *Street Life in London.*

Thomson's humanism had another dimension, the desire to share the hard-won vision. In the introduction to *Through China with Camera,* however, he spoke for two generations of pioneering photographers:

> "The camera has always been the companion of my travels and has supplied the only accurate means . . . to share . . . the scenes and people of far-off lands."

* *The Heads of Executed Criminals* is an obvious exception to this mood.

NOTES:

INTRODUCTION

1. Helmut and Alison Gernsheim, *L. J. M. Daguerre: the History of the Diorama and the Daguerreotype,* New York: Dover Publication, Inc., 1968, p. 85. (republication of 1956 first edition, Martin Secker and Warburg, London.)
2. André Jammes, Robert Sobieszek and Minor White, *French Primitive Photography,* New York: Aperture, Inc., 1970. quotation from Sobieszek's *Historical Commenatary,* pages unnumbered.
3. Susan Sontag, *On Photography,* New York: Farrar, Straus and Giroux, 1977, p. 3.

"THE BRITISH PHOTOGRAPHER ABROAD"

1. Dr. Thomas, director of the Science Museum, London, private communication.
2. Aaron Scharf, *Art and Photography,* Harmondsworth: Penguin Books Ltd., 1975, pp. 104-5.
3. Gail Buckland, private communication and description of a calotype of Orleans Cathedral in the Talbot exhibition held at the Pierpont Morgan Library, New York, 1979.
4. Author unknown, "The Application of the Talbotype," *The Art Union,* July, 1846, p. 195.
5. *Ibid,* p. 195.
6. H. J. P. Arnold, *William Henry Fox Talbot: Pioneer of Photography and Man of Science,* London: Hutchinson Benham, 1977, p. 149.
7. Author unknown, "A Reminiscence of the Calotype Club," *British Journal of Photography,* August 14, 1874, p. 385.
8. *Calotypes by D. O. Hill and R. Adamson Selected from his Collection by Andrew Elliott,* Edinburgh: privately printed, 1928. John Millar Gray, "The Early History of Photography," (being the introduction though written c. 1885), p. 4.
9. Sir John Herschel, note from the catalogue of the Photographic Society's first exhibition, 1854.
10. Jammes, Sobieszek and White, *op. cit.,* quotation from White's *Introduction.*
11. Ray Desmond, "Photography in India in the Nineteenth Century," *India Office Library and Records: Report for the Year 1974,* p. 13.
12. Francis Frith, "Early Morning, Wady Kardassy," *Egypt and Palestine Photographed and Described,* Vol. I, London: James Virtue, 1859.
13. Hippolyte Taine quoted by Elizabeth Lindquist-Cock, *The Influence of Photography on American Landscape Painting, 1839-1880,* New York and London: Garland Publishing Inc., 1977, p. 7.
14. R. G. Collingwood, *The Idea of History,* New York: Oxford University Press, 1956, p. 133.
15. Felicity Ashbee, "William Carrick: A Scots Photographer in St. Petersburg 1827-1878)," *History of Photography,* July, 1978, pp. 207-223.
16. Weston Naef, *Era of Exploration: The Rise of Landscape Photography in the American West, 1860-1885,* Buffalo and New York: Albright-Knox Gallery and The Metropolitan Museum of Art, 1975, p. 170.
17. Desmond, *op. cit.,* p. 24.

OTHER SOURCES:

BOOKS AND ARTICLES

Gail Buckland, *Reality Recorded: Early Documentary Photography, Greenwich, Conn:* New York Graphic Society, 1974.

Nigel Cameron, *The Face of China: As Seen by Photographers & Travelers, 1860 - 1912,* Millerton, New York: Aperture, Inc.

Gilberto Ferrez and Weston Naef, *Pioneer Photographers of Brazil 1840-1912,* New York: The Center for Inter-American Relations, 1976.

Helmut Gernsheim, *The History of Photography,* New York: McGraw-Hill Book Company, 1969.
Roger Fenton: Photographer of the Crimean War, London: Secker & Warburg, 1954.

Ralph Greenhill and Andrew Birrell, *Canadian Photography 1839-1920, Toronto:* The Coach House Press, 1979.

John Hanavy, *Roger Fenton of Crimble Hall,* London: Gordon Fraser, 1975.

Clark Woswick, *The Last Empire: Photography in British India,* 1855-1911, London: Gordon Fraser, 1976.
Imperial China: Photographs 1850-1912, New York: Pennwick Publishing, Inc., 1978.

Samuel Bourne, "Ten Weeks with Camera in the Himalayas," *British Journal of Photography,* February 1, 1864, pp. 50-51 and February 15, 1864, p. 69.
"Narrative of a Photographic Trip to Kashmir (Cashmere) and adjacent Areas," *British Journal of Photography,* published in parts, from October 5, 1866 to February 8, 1867.
"A Photographic Journey through the Higher Himalayas," *British Journal of Photography,* published in parts, from November 26, 1869 to March 4, 1870.

Isabelle Jammes, "Louis-Désiré Blanquart-Evrard 1802-1872," *Camera,* December, 1978.

G. Thomas, "The First Four Decades of Photography in India," *History of Photography,* July, 1979, pp. 215-227.

APPENDIX:

Abstract of Foreign Travel Photographs by Britons taken from Four Exhibition Catalogues of the 1850's

from "A Catalogue of an Exhibition of Recent Specimens of Photography Exhibited at the House of the Society of Arts, 18 John Street, Adelphi" (The exhibition, held from December 1852 - January 1853, had 779 exhibits, several of these having more than one image.)

Roger Fenton	Russia	3	waxed paper
Peter Wickens Fry	France	9	calotype
R. C. Galton	France	5	calotype
John Stewart	France	3	calotype

from "Photographic Society: Exhibition of Photographs and Daguerreotypes at the Gallery of the Society of British Artists, Suffolk Street, Pall Mall. First Year." (The exhibition, held from January - February 1854, had 839 exhibits, several of these having more than one image.)

Frederick W. Berger	Australia	1	wet collodion
P. Bird	Egypt and Spain	35	waxed paper
J. C. Bourne	Russia	2	waxed paper
Charles Clifford	Spain	6	albumenized prints from calotypes
W. T. Collings	Belgium	1	negative unspecified
George Edwards	France	1	daguerreotype
Roger Fenton	Russia	36	waxed paper (35), wet collodion (1)
Peter Wickens Fry	France	1	wet collodion
J. Martin	France	1	negative unspecified
Hon. Phipps	Italy	3	daguerreotypes
E. K. Tenison	Spain	4	waxed paper
Jas. West	France	1	calotype

from "Photographic Society: Exhibition of Photographs and Daguerreotypes at the Gallery of the Society of Water Colour Painters, 5 Pall Mall East. Second Year." (The exhibiton, held from January - February 1855, had 768 exhibits, several of these having more than one image.)

James Anderson	Italy	4	albumen on glass
Arthur Backhouse	France and Italy	9	waxed paper
J. C. Bourne	Russia	15	calotype
Dr. Hugh Welch Diamond	Portugal	3	calotype
J. J. Forester	Portugal	1	calotype
Capt. Holder	France	2	waxed paper
Maxwell Lyte	France	8	wet collodion
Hugh Owen	Portugal	9	calotype
James Roberston	Turkey	20	wet collodion
J. A. Silk	France	1	wet collodion
John Stewart	France	4	wet paper process
E. K. Tenison	France	10	calotype (5) waxed paper (5)
W. A. West	France	6	calotype

from "Photographic Society: Exhibition of Photographs and Daguerreotypes at the South Kensington Museum. London, 1858. Fifth Year." (705 exhibits.)

Francis Bedford	Germany	11	wet collodion
T. Coddington	Belgium	1	waxed paper
Francis Frith	Egypt and Palestine	16	wet collodion
William M. Grundy	Egypt and Turkey	5	wet collodion
Frank Haes	Australia	7	waxed paper
R. Hall	Australia	1	positive on glass
Rev. Percy Lousada	Spain	1	wet paper process
Serg. Mack, R. E.	Russia	?	negative unspecified
Dr. Mansell	France	1	syrup collodion
Corp. Miliken, R.E.	Singapore	?	negative unspecified
Dr. John Murray	India	8	waxed paper
T. E. Nightengale	France	1	calotype
Rev. S. M. Raven	France	2	waxed paper
G. R. Smith	Belgium	5	dry collodion
C. Thurston Thompson	France	1	wet collodion
Benjamin Brecknell Turner	Holland	4	calotype

GLOSSARY:

Some Technical Terms Defined

Daguerreotype: Made public in 1839, Daguerre's invention, the first practical photographic process, produced a unique image on a polished, silver coated copper plate. Reacting with iodine and bromine vapours, the silvered surface formed a light sensitive halide. After being exposed in a camera, the plate was developed over a dish of heated mercury, making visible the latent image, and then fixed in a bath of sodium thiosulfate.

Paper Negatives: The main advantage of Talbot's *calotype* process, patented in 1841, was that multiple prints could be made from a single negative. (Strictly speaking the term refers only to the negative, though a salted paper print made from such a negative is commonly described as being a calotype.) After being coated with a solution of silver nitrate and potassium iodide, then dried, a piece of fine writing paper was brushed with solutions of silver nitrate and gallic acid. The paper could be exposed dry or wet *(the wet paper process),* then developed by a solution of gallo-nitrate of silver, rinsed and fixed. Preparation, exposure and development had to be carried out on the same day. To increase translucency and reduce printing time, the negative was then waxed. The *waxed paper negative,* Gustav Le Gray's improvement of 1851, involved waxing the paper at the start of the process, before any chemicals were applied. Much finer detail could be obtained and the paper could be prepared up to ten days before use and developed a few days after exposure.

Glass negatives: The *albumen-on-glass negative,* introduced by Niepce de Saint-Victor in 1848, provided much finer detail than the calotype and the plate could be prepared long in advance and be developed up to two weeks after exposure. A glass plate was coated with potassium iodide and albumen, dried and then sensitized with a silver nitrate solution; after exposure it was developed with gallic acid and fixed. The *wet collodion* process, made public by Frederick Scott Archer in 1851, because of the sharpness of its detail and shortness of its exposure, supplanted all other processes by 1860. A glass plate coated with potassium iodide and collodion (gun cotton dissolved in ether, which forms a tough transparent membrane) was dipped into a solution of silver nitrate, exposed while wet and developed immediately. As on site preparation was often inconvenient and wet collodion became useless if not used immediately, various methods, known collectively as *dry collodion,* evolved for keeping the plate sensitive. MacPherson used the *collodio-albumen* process, introduced in 1855, in which a collodion plate was coated with iodized albumen, given a second silver nitrate bath and then dried, to be used up to several weeks later. In the *syrup collodion* process, the prepared plate was kept moist and sensitive by coating it with a solution of honey and distilled water.

Paper Positives: The *salted paper print* or *salt print* was made public by Talbot in 1839. Paper soaked in a salt solution and sensitized with silver nitrate was then exposed to daylight under a negative — the two held together in a printing frame — until an image of sufficient density appeared; then the photograph was washed and fixed. The print might then have been coated with a layer of varnish or albumen *(albumenized salt print)* to give the surface vitality. By developing his prints chemically, instead of the usual physical printing-out process, Blanquart-Evrard was able to reduce the exposure time to a few seconds, allowing his Lille factory to mass produce fine photographic prints, which were given two hypo baths, toned with gold chloride and washed thoroughly *(Blanquart-Evrard process print).* Blanquart-Evrard also invented *albumen paper,* whereby the printing paper was coated with a solution of albumen and salt, then sensitized with silver nitrate. The smooth, glossy surface was perfectly suited to the detail and sharpness of glass negatives.

Other Processes (Used in Book Illustration)

Using the principle that bichromate of potash loses its solubility in water in proportion to its exposure to light — and this being also true for organic substances mixed with the bichromate — Alphonse Poitevin, in 1855, invented the collotype and carbon print for producing photographic images. In the *collotype* process, a sheet of stone or glass was coated with the bichromate, exposed under a negative and washed with water. The exposed parts accept a greasy printer's ink in proportion to the amount of light they have received. Poitevin's *carbon print* process was perfected in 1864 by Joseph Swan with the invention of carbon tissue, a film of gelatine with finely powdered carbon, which was produced commercially in 1866. The tissue was sensitized by the operator with bichromate and exposed under a negative. The face of the tissue was attached to a temporary paper support, soaked in hot water and then the back pulled away and the soluble gelatine dissolved. As the image was laterally reversed, the tissue had to be transferred to a final paper support and the temporary backing peeled away.

ACKNOWLEDGEMENTS

I would first like to express my gratitude to Mrs. Jeanette Jackson, director of the Camden Arts Centre, for sponsoring an exhibition in which I was given free rein to present formally my obsession with the beauty and power of early travel photography, a concern of the past three years and still seen through a glass darkly. I would next like to thank Mrs. Carolyn Bloore, whose research brought to light the exhibition catalogues of the 1850's, obvious treasures of information, which to date have somehow eluded serious examination by historians of photography, and for all her advice on matters technical.

For making reproductions from their photographic collections available, I thank Miss Katherine Lloyd and Mr. John Ward of the Science Museum for plates 1, 2 and 5; and Mr. Antony Burnett-Brown and Mr. Robert Lassam of the Fox Talbot Museum for plates 4, 7 and 8. My gratitude to the trusting souls who provided original prints for reproduction: The Photographic Society of Ireland, especially Mr. Peater Slattery and Mr. Edward Chandler, for plates 12 - 13; Miss Sara Stevenson and Mr. R. E. Hutchison of the Scottish National Portrait Gallery for plates 14 - 17; Mr. William Reid and Mrs. Harding of the National Army Museum for plates 19 - 20; Mr. Paul Walter for plate 23; Mr. Robert Koch for plate 24; Mr. and Mrs. Taylor for plates 29, 43 and 44; Mr. Alan Paviot for plate 38; Mr. Peter Coffeen for plate 40; Mr. Mark Haworth-Booth of the Victoria and Albert Museum for plates 44 - 45; Mr. Willem DiePraam for plate 63; and Mr. Daniel Wolf for plate 69. (All other plates have been reproduced from original prints in the author's collection.) And special thanks to the staff of the Edinburgh Public Library who made the *Calotype Club Album* so readily available.

For all their encouragement, advice and information, I thank Ms. Gail Buckland, Mr. Ray Desmond of the India Records Office Library, Mr. Robert Lassam of the Fox Talbot Museum, Mr. David Shaw Smith, Miss Sara Stevenson of the Scottish National Portrait Gallery and Dr. D. B. Thomas of the Science Museum; my colleagues from Paris, Mr. Gerard Levy and Mr. Alan Paviot; and my friends in photography, Els Barents, Richard Brettell, Keith Collie, Willem DiePraam, Heather Forbes, Philippe Garner, Judy Goldhill, Ken Jacobsen, Robert Koch, Ian Moor, Catherine Saunders, Helena Srakocic and Keith and Usha Taylor. My deepest appreciation to my wife Paula for removing a multitude of errors from the text, for so bravely suffering me through the extended crisis surrounding the book and the exhibition and for our son, Jesse.